Following TMMi practices to produce Quality software products

TMMi practices following in software testing projects for incremental process improvement

Author: Shanthi Vemulapalli

Version 1.0

Copyright 2015

Preface

Every Software project need to follow the certain industry processes and the standards to get the quality products for any business operations. While planning for these processes adoption, one needs to think whether they can be used strategically to produce the quality software by having incremental process improvements.

When the management pursues such kind of thoughts, Test Maturity Model Integration is one of the famous processes integration package in parallel to CMMi.

The TMMi has been getting popular due to its detailed specific process areas and it has easy adoptable capabilities. I have used TMM and TMMi in many of my previous projects for different customers around the world for different business domain areas through my past services rendered to IT services companies.

While planning for implementation we need to get the management commitment also where they agree to adopt incremental process improvements to gain the software quality incrementally.

Without having; the resources trained and motivated continuously and constantly by getting their commitment, it is impossible to implement a new setup. Hence the management also needs to understand the test organization setup needs and its continuous improvements.

At the same time the development team also needs to adopt some of the CMMi processes in parallel to the TMMi processes. Then only through both the teams it is possible to have the roadmap for incremental quality software programme implementation.

I felt to share the TMMi implementation knowledge to the global IT professionals to impart this kind of motivation and the practices for their IT organizations. As a part of my initial thought I started this Book to present to the audience.

In this book I have given the need of having CMMi and TMMi in practice along with their processes. And I have planned to educate the professionals incrementally by considering from Level2 process areas onwards. Initially I have considered; "Test Policy and Strategy" which is under TMMi level2, in this book to expand their importance and the usage with live examples. You can keep looking for other books those contain the remaining process areas for Level2. Without having the Level2 processes in practices it is not advisable to consider other levels of TMMi.

Table of contents

Chapter1: Introduction

Chapter2:TMMi and supporting CMMi KPAs

Chapter3:TMMi Level1 [Initial]

Chapter4: TMMi Level2 process areas

Chapter5: TMMi Level2 Test Policy and Strategy

Chapter6: TMMi Level2 Establish a Test Strategy

Chapter7: TMMi Level2: Establish Test Performance Indicators

Conclusion

About the author

Other publications: by Shanthi Vemulapalli

Chapter1: Introduction

Testing profession is a competitive and challenging activity in front of the software development and business groups.

The testing professional needs to learn incrementally not only the application functionalities; the latest trends towards improving the testing process incrementally and also to learn the applications relevant technology; is essential. Timely these updates bring them their bread and butter also to survive in the IT industry.

While thinking and digging about the testing process improvements techniques or models; Test Maturity Model Integration is becoming very popular. And most of the organizations and the testing professionals are looking towards on it.

As per the current Testing practices trend; most of the IT organizations or departments they are following the Test Maturity Models integration [TMMi] practices to control the products or projects defects and also to bring the process improvements towards SDLC and Test life cycle.

Within my 25 plus years of global IT professional experience I have involved 15 plus years in QA and testing profession. I could use these practices in many projects to bring out the quality products delivery to the customers. Some of the benefits are tangible to the customers. Later on they could recognize the intangible benefits under long term.

I also found in my past projects globally at different locations with different customers; many people could not follow the process steps unless somebody denote an example to them either by a proof of concept activity or implemented in their projects. This experience brought me a thought of sharing the past knowledge through a book.

Through this E-Book I thought I can share the some of the TMMi practices implementation thoughts for different KPAs , their sub-processes and practices. Also let us note the reader is supposed to be aware of the TMMi Levels and their process areas before reading this book.

The reader is advised to go through the website: www.tmmifoundation.org for its framework and other guidelines from the PDF document: "The overall structure of the TMMi Reference Model including details of each level."

The reader is also need to realize this E-Book is going to help to give a thought process on how to co-relate or implement a particular TMMi sub-process in their project or organization with examples. For every Process area of sub-process they need to refer the TMMi framework book from the foundation site. That has been considered as a guide while elaborating the process steps in this book with examples.

I would like to denote the KPAs through high level process charts or figures drawn by me, against to each KPA while moving to co-relate them for live examples.

Chapter2:TMMi and supporting CMMi KPAs

As per the TMMi framework; the organization or the project which is going to be applied with TMMi should be following the CMMi KPAs. Hence the reader need to be aware of the SDLC process of the project for which the TMMi practices are going to be applied for.

At the same time the SDLC team need to follow the relevant CMMi KPAs towards their software engineering practices.

Initially; I would like to recollect the KPAs involved in TMMi

and the supporting CMMi

KPAs at different levels from the below figure:

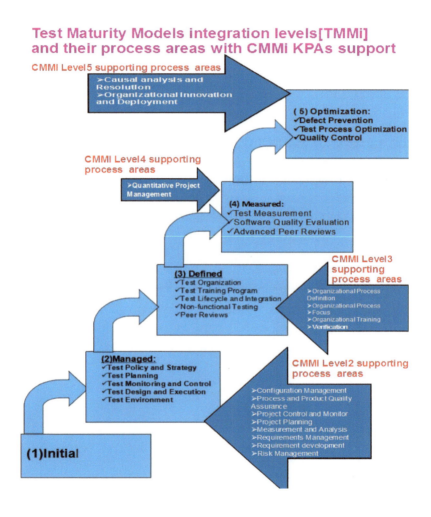

Chapter3:TMMi Level1 [Initial]

Eventhough the TMMi framework do not consider Level1 as a practices; we as professionals need to be aware of the situations we can smell in the organizations those can come under Level1.

Example:

I have considered some of the conversation symptoms of the Level1 and drawn them under a chart with the below representation:

Level1: Some of the symptomps for denoting testing is a chaotic

The conversation environment for Undefined process:

Developer:
As a developer I do not have requirement in hand.
I have completed the coding and you can test in developer machine.
I do not like this test technic.Use a monkey testing method.

Test engineer:
No test data I used some of the junk characters to keyin the data.

Developer:
Ooh sorry my dear tester, I gave you a wrong file to test it.
Let me put the right file from my pen drive.

Test engineer:
As a tester I have done my testing from the developer machine.
It is working fine and it can be deployed in production.

User:
I tried to keyin the data it is displaying messages like "Testing field1", "Now pass to next loop"

Developer:
Sorry my dear user; I forgot to remove my code debug messages.

User:
Dear tester have you not seen these messages while testing.

Test engineer:
Ooh; it is the developer machine. I thouht for him it should display the same messages.

User:
Guys! please get the right file to my production box in next three hours.
I am loosing my customers. I need to issue the customer ids.

Developer:
ooh! I will definitely remove those messages.

Test engineer:
I will verify the new file again and confirm you.

With the above conversations; the experienced testing professional might catch the Lack of test environment, Lack of development process and standards, lack of testing documentation and standards following, lack of requirements management process, etc.

If you recollect the CMMI Supporting KPAs under Level2; none of them are present in the above example. It is the environment where one or more people like to do just to complete the job, without having a proper process in place. And also there is a lack of self education in each of the above roles.

Chapter4: TMMi Level2 Managed process areas

Now, let us move forward for Level2 of TMMi. It has the following process areas:

- ➢ Test Policy and Strategy
- ➢ Test Planning
- ➢ Test Monitoring and Control
- ➢ Test Design and Execution
- ➢ Test Environment

Each Process area has its sub-processes. These have been

clubbed together and drawn into the following chart:

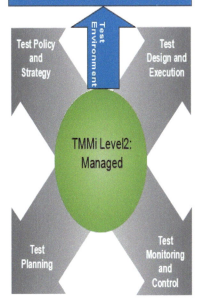

Now let us consider each of the main process areas and study their feasibility of implementation in typical testing organization.

Example:

With reference to the above sub-process steps, we need to consider several areas to define the examples for each sub-process area. We may not be able to connect among the examples. At this point let us assume and independent example for each of the sub-process areas, wherever it is considered for connecting those can be referred for a discussion.

Chapter5: TMMi Level2 Test Policy and Strategy

As per the TMMi framework definition, "A test policy, aligned with the business (quality) policy, is established and agreed upon by the stakeholders."

The size of the policies can vary from one organization to another depends on different parameters. Sometimes it is related with the organization's Quality and other policies also. In this section, I have taken a simple example to explain. But the reader can convert into their project needs.

As we have seen the example in Level1, in such situations a test policy and Strategy is very essential to deploy the quality product into production. We can consider the same example on how to apply the level 2 processes to improve the testing process for this project or organization.

As per the framework definition, this process area has three sub-processes as below:

"Define test goals, Define test policy, Distribute the test policy to stakeholders."

Following chart can give them as a reference for reader's future recollection:

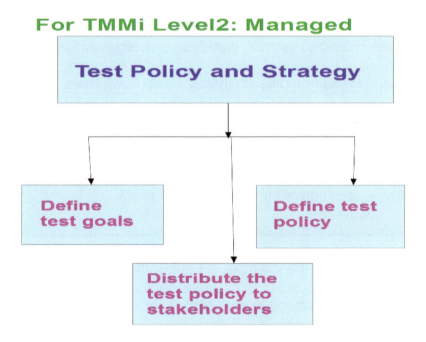

Now let us consider these sub-processes implementation to improve them.

As per the framework document, let us recollect their definitions:

Define test goals: It is defined as "Define and maintain test goals based upon business needs and objectives."

Example for Test goals:

From the Level1 example. The project needs to have test goals.

As an example; if we consider a new Bank ATM operation. It test goals are: Requirement can be "The ATM machine need to accept the ATM Cards of any Bank. The business need to support all the ATM cards of recognized Banks".

Simple; test goal can be "Test the ATM machine with right and wrong Cards. Test ATM with non-recognized bank cards also".

Assuming in your project you have defined the test goals as your business requires and they have been agreed by the business.

Define test policy:

As per the definition; "A test policy, aligned with the business (quality) policy, is defined based on the test goals and agreed upon by the stakeholders."

Let us assume the users of Bank wanted to have a Quality policy like; "All the applications should be tested in a pre-production environment before deployment into production.". And this was agreed by the project sponsor, other heads. Now let us see the below example.

Example for Test policy:

With reference to the business users Quality policy the testing team can divide it into their teams internal operational requirement.

"The application Testing team needs to test all applications in the Pre-UAT environment. This environment should have all the production applications and their latest data."

It denotes the Test team's internal test policy with reference to the Business user's Quality policy.

Distribute the test policy to stakeholders: As per the definition "The test policy and test goals are presented and explained to stakeholders inside and outside testing."

All the test policies defined by the testing teams should be circulated to all the relevant units or departments, to know the internal policies how they have been laid down to comply with the other policies.

Similar way the relevant Testing project or organization can have multiple policies related to; Testing team, Rules to be followed in testing, Process improvement guidelines, Role performance, Assets or resources handling or usage, Security, etc. Once they are defined within the testing team they should be circulated to the stakeholders for their awareness. A walkthrough session or call is suggested with the stakeholders.

Chapter6: TMMi Level2 Establish a Test Strategy

As per the definition; "An organization-wide or program-wide test strategy that identifies and defines the test levels to be performed is established and deployed.".

In any organization many software products can be there under re-engineering or new development. Each of them might have a different business goals and features. The test test strategy need to be defined with relevant to the specific product or a group of products those have common business goal.

Example:

In a Financial institution like a Bank; might have lot of Telecommunication or network related products. They all need to have specific hardware and external or/and internal software. While defining test strategies, each of the products or sub-products should have different test scenarios. With those scenarios; they should have different environments, etc. and the test strategies should be different obviously. And these will be applied with relation to the specific product business goals.

In the same Bank, apart from the above product category; there can be ERP applications and Core Banking applications also. These all can come into in-house developed software categories. They all will have specific business goals. Then the strategies also will vary.

This Process area is divided into three categories of sub-processes. i.e;

Perform a generic product risk assessment, Define test strategy and distribute the test strategy to stakeholders.

Following chart can give them as a reference for reader's future recollection:

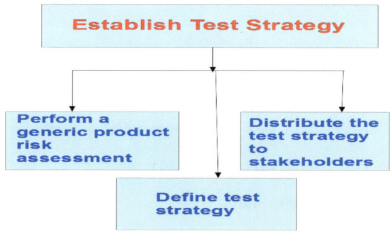

For TMMi Level2: Test Policy and Strategy

Establish Test Strategy

Perform a generic product risk assessment

Distribute the test strategy to stakeholders

Define test strategy

How to perform a generic product risk assessment:

The purpose is; "A generic product risk assessment is

performed to identify the typical critical areas for testing."

We have seen in the above example of banking operation with different products with different business goals. And their variation of test strategies. When these are considered for testing; there can be risks for building or handling test environment, network, infrastructure, even an in-experienced test engineer also can create risk for testing. We may find similar kind of generic risks while planning for products testing. These risks need to be listed and the products need to be assessed towards eliminating the risks by involving the relevant teams along with the stakeholders.

How to Define test strategy:

As per the definition; "The test strategy is defined that identifies and defines the test levels. For each level, the objectives, responsibilities, main tasks, entry/exit criteria and so forth are defined."

Example:

We can consider the Bank applications example. We have analyzed on products test strategies and the risks. The same way we need to identify the levels of [Unit, Integration, System, User acceptance] testing, the test objectives, Responsibilities of testing team or engineers, the main tasks involved, The test entry criteria and exit criteria need to be defined. When we have these contents in place it will be clear for every contributor and also to the stakeholders. Many risks can be identified and they can be reduced or nullified also.

How to distribute the test strategy to stakeholders:

As per the framework guidelines; *"The test strategy is presented to and discussed with stakeholders inside and outside testing."*

As we have seen in "Distribute the test policy to stakeholders:". Similar way the test strategy and risks need to be defined and circulated to stakeholders. And organize a presentation session for their easy understanding or to have on the same page across the programme. This can eliminate the future conflicts also.

Chapter7: TMMi Level2: Establish Test Performance Indicators

As per definition; "*A set of goal-oriented test process performance indicators to measure the quality of the test process is established and deployed.*"

Example:

From the above examples we have seen the test levels, entry and exit criteria towards defining the strategies. Assuming that there are different teams of the test engineers; for Unit test, Integration testing, System Testing, Acceptance testing. For each phase or levels of testing there have been defined entry and exit criteria. The performance of the testing activities needs to be defined at this process level.

It has three sub-processes; Define test performance indicators and Deploy test performance indicators.

The below figure depicts them.

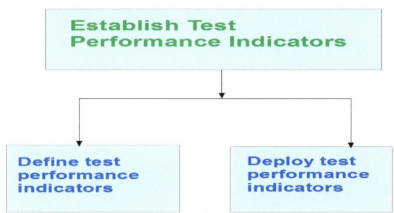

How to Define test performance indicators?:

As per the definition; "*The test performance indicators are defined based upon the test policy and goals, including a procedure for data collection, storage and analysis.*"

From the Banking products example; Let us assume the user group or some of the stake holders do not want the product to be deployed unless it is passed for a group of features with a specific production [business] data. This is an indicator to perform the activity by the team and to identify the performance of the product. At the same time the acceptance test should not have started unless the exit criteria of all the previous levels of the tests are met. This is also an indicator to complete all the levels of the tests to assess the product to pass to Acceptance test.

How to Deploy test performance indicators?:

As per the definition; "Deploy the test performance indicators and provide measurement results for the identified test performance indicators to stakeholders."

The relevant product test policies can have the performance indicators documented. When the test results are produced, it can be measured.

Example:

In every testing organization, there are regular reporting methods either through tools or by documentation. Through them one can know the test performance indicators.

Conclusion:

By following the above practices with the given feasible example scenarios one can implement these practices in their testing projects incrementally to gain the software quality acceleration. Let us have a common understanding no new process can be implemented overnight. It need some time to groom the resources, build the test organization by incorporating lot of policies, procedures, standards and processes. Then the internal motivation is also need to be accelerated the speed of the teams. Mainly the management continuous and constant support is required along with the relevant budget. Then the test management can step down to prove the implementation of these best practices incrementally with dedication and long term commitments. If you are satisfied with my elaborations on the specific processes, please look for my other process area books under TMMi level2.

About the author

Shanthi Kumar Vemulapalli is a seasoned professional with 25+ years of global IT experience in cost-effectively utilizing technology in alignment with corporate goals. Delivered bottom-line ITSM results through competent project and program management solutions, successful development and execution of systems, and implementation of best practices. He worked in different BI evaluation phases for more than 10 plus years for different business and technologies domain areas along with 15 years of his involvement in QA/Testing projects.

Recognized for inculcating a culture of innovation and knowledge sharing in organizations. Built teams for many companies globally; through training, mentoring and guiding the IT resources along with the on project competencies building. Supported for many infrastructure setups and conversion related projects [onsite/offshore model].

His Professional Certifications: ITIL V3 Expert Certification –
Service Lifecycle, PRINCE2 Practitioner Certification, Lean
Six Sigma Black Belt, Cloud computing Foundation [EXIN] and
Certified Tester Foundation Level [CTFL].

He also wrote several blogs on the IT related topics. They are
available in the below blog sites:

1. http://vskumarblogs.wordpress.com/

2. http://vskumarcloudblogs.wordpress.com/

3. http://vskumar35.wordpress.com/

Other publications: by Shanthi Vemulapalli

1. Test planning with TMMi practices
2. How to control cost for IT services - Startup company
3. Testing BI and ETL Applications with manual and
   automation approach

4. Data migration testing practice

5. Startup IT Business Ideas: How to strategize your
   services through ITIL V3 Service Strategy?

6. IT services Design and practices for IT Startup Company

7. IT services Design and practices for IT Startup Company

From the following link also you can see his publications:

http://www.amazon.com/-/e/B018EDQTX6